MY BROTHER IS A PREEMIE

A Children's Guide to the NICU Experience

Written by Joseph A. Vitterito II MD

Illustrated by Abraham R. Chuzzlewit

About the illustrator.
Abraham R. Chuzzlewit is a relatively new children's book author and illustrator. His style has been described as nonsensical, yet brilliant and sometimes lovingly acerbic. He tends to cover topics close to the hearts of children with a whimsically simple perspective.

Besides writing and illustrating, he takes exorbitantly long naps, wrestles rambunctiously with his siblings, and occasionally eats soap.

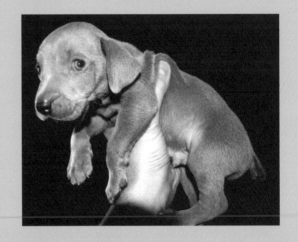

Yup! I was a very small pup!

ISBN 9780988294028
Text copyright ©2012
Illustration copyright ©2012
LCCN 2012952849

Written and illustrated by Joseph A. Vitterito II MD (Abraham R. Chuzzlewit)
www.brysontaylorpublishing.com/chuzzlewit

Published by
Bryson Taylor Publishing
199 New County Road
Saco, ME 04072
www.brysontaylorpublishing.com

An innocent heart holds the most knowledge and speaks the most truth.

For Samuel J. Tinkerton and all those like him.

Foreword by the author.

For everyone involved, having an infant in the Neonatal Intensive Care Unit is full of a flurry of emotions overshadowed by anxiety. An admission to the NICU is not anticipated and therefore can be a very trying experience.

Explaining the hospitalization of the baby to the other children in your home can be challenging. The baby's siblings may be too young to understand, fearful of hospitals, or even upset that you are spending more time at the hospital than at home.

This short book can serve as a light introduction to the NICU and foster further discussion with your other children or young relatives. It is best read together, ideally before a visit to the NICU. In addition to visiting the hospital, establish some routines and alone time with your children at home to help ease the transition as your new baby grows and heals in the intensive care unit.

Also, talk with the staff at the hospital and your Primary Care provider for other helpful suggestions as you and your family cope with having a loved one in neonatal intensive care.

Jos. A Vitterito II MD is a Neonatologist at Maine Medical Center in Portland, Maine. He attended Dartmouth Medical School, completed residency in General Pediatrics at Brown University/Hasbro Children's Hospital, and fellowship in Neonatal/Perinatal Medicine at Dartmouth Hitchcock Medical Center. Additionally, he serves as the Medical Director at Rhode Island School for the Deaf in Providence, Rhode Island.

He would like to acknowledge all the terrific inspiration and teaching of his past and present mentors and colleagues at Women & Infants' Hospital, Dartmouth Medical School/Dartmouth-Hitchcock Medical Center, and Maine Medical Center.

MY BROTHER IS A PREEMIE
AND I HEARD HE'S VERY TEENY.
HE HAS TO STAY IN A HOSPITAL.
LET ME TELL YOU ABOUT IT ALL.

HE HAS TINY HANDS & FEET,
LITTLE FINGERS
AND
ITSY BITSY TOES.

HE'S SOMEONE
I CAN'T WAIT TO MEET,
BUT I CAN'T HOLD HIM UNTIL HE
GROWS!

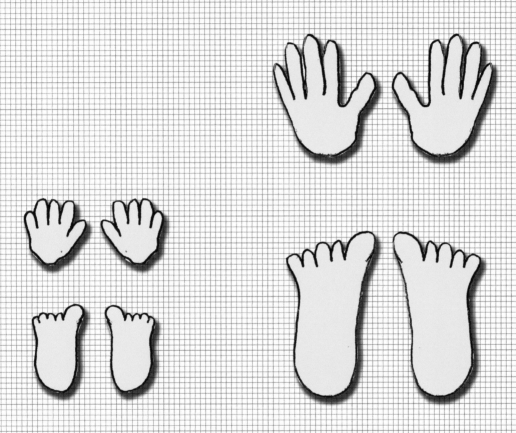

HE HAS TO STAY
IN A SPECIAL BED.
IT KEEPS HIM
SAFE & WARM.
I HAVE TO
TALK SOFTLY,
THEY SAID.
SO THAT
STRONGER
HE CAN BECOME.

HE HAS A MACHINE
TO HELP HIM BREATHE
THROUGH HIS MOUTH OR NOSE.
IN AND OUT OF HIS LITTLE BODY
THE CLEAN FRESH AIR GOES.

HE HAS HIS OWN
SPECIAL TELEVISION
WITH ALL KINDS OF
NUMBERS & COLORS.

IT FLASHES BRIGHT
WHEN HE NEEDS ATTENTION
AND IN COME
THE NURSES & DOCTORS.

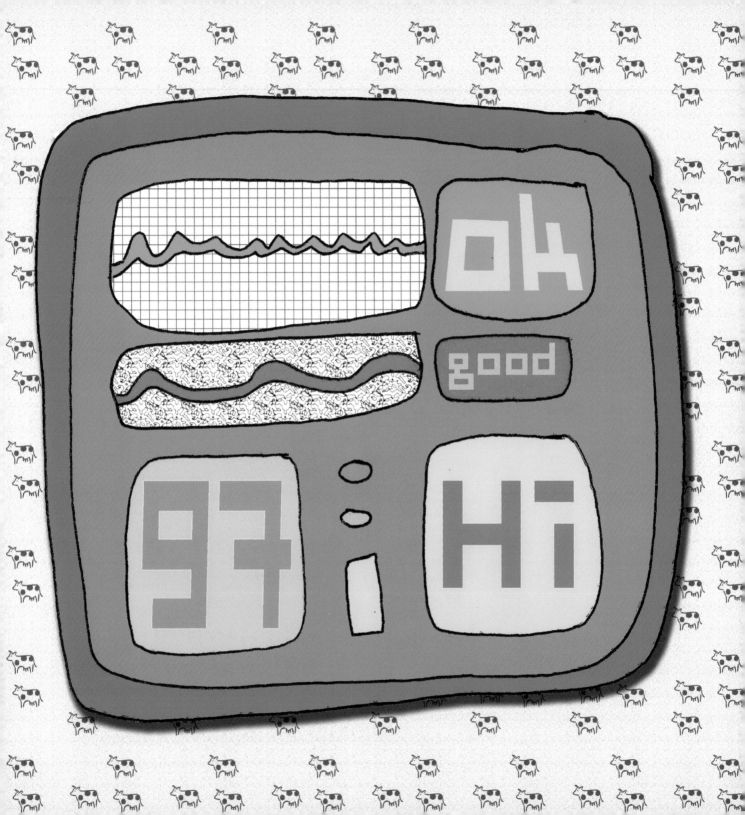

HE'S WAY TOO SMALL
TO EAT EASILY
SO HE HAS A SOFT TUBE
IN HIS NOSE.

FROM THERE TO
HIS LITTLE ROUND BELLY,
ALL THE SPECIAL MILK GOES.

SOME OF HIS MACHINES MAKE A LOT OF NOISE:

BEEPS BUZZES & BINGS!!!

HIS ROOM HAS
SPECIAL LIGHTS, TOO.
TODAY IT WAS ALL BLUE!

WOW!
THE THINGS IN THIS PLACE
MAKE ME FEEL LIKE I'M IN
OUTER SPACE!

THE HOSPITAL IS REALLY
NOT SUCH A SCARY PLACE

AND I GOT TO SEE
THE LITTLE GUY'S FACE!

NOW I KNOW WHY
HE HAS TO STAY.

STILL,
I CAN'T WAIT UNTIL HE CAN
COME HOME AND PLAY!

NICUISMS

A Primer for Parents

VENTILATOR

This machine helps babies who need help with breathing. Many different kinds of ventilators are available. The concept is all the same: providing oxygen to the lungs and taking carbon dioxide out. "Weaning" from a ventilator means slowly reducing the amount of help the ventilator provides as the baby's lungs become stronger and healthier.

MONITOR

This keeps track of the baby's breathing, heart rate, blood pressure, how much oxygen is in the blood (the "sat"), and various other signs of the baby's health.

BILI LIGHT

Bilirubin lights provide phototherapy for jaundiced babies. Some of these lights shine a bright blue light and some are plain light. They both do the same thing: breaking down the extra bilirubin in the skin. These lights do not cause sunburn but your baby will need to wear protective eyewear while treated.

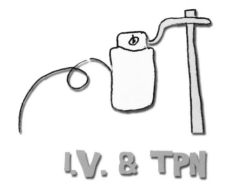

I.V. & TPN

An IV bag can hold many different kinds of solutions. A basic IV solution usually contains sugars, salts and minerals necessary to keep the baby's body in balance. Some solutions called "TPN" have additional nutrients for the baby including fat and protein. These solutions are substitutes for food until the baby is able to tolerate food in his or her belly. IV lines are placed in the same places as adults. Additionally, sometimes we place IV catheters in the vessels in the baby's belly button.

ISOLETTE

These modern-day units serve many purposes for premature infants: protection, warmth, and quiet. Some monitor the infant's temperature and automatically adjust the "thermostat." Some of these units have tops which lift up and some have doors or inlets on the sides which swing open. By the way, we don't call them "incubators" anymore... we left that term on some chicken farm back in the seventies!

FEEDING TUBE

Premature babies are unable to coordinate feedings well. Nasogastric ("NG") and orogastric ("OG") tubes are made of a soft material. These tubes are passed from either the baby's nose (NG) or mouth (OG) into the stomach in order to administer nutritious breast milk or formula directly into your baby's belly. We call these "enteral" feedings (as opposed to "parenteral" which means through an IV). As your baby learns to eat directly, we slowly reduce the amount he or she receives through the tube.

this story was inspired by the creative creatures at

bah! h umdogs!

CPSIA information can be obtained at www.ICGtesting.com
Printed in the USA
BVIW12n1223270615
406430BV00002B/2